We Can Do That!

100+ Ways Families Can Be On Mission

Tonya W. Heartsill

Birmingham, Alabama

Woman's Missionary Union, SBC
P. O. Box 830010
Birmingham, AL 35283-0010

For more information, visit our Web site at www.wmu.com or call
1-800-968-7301.

Dewey Decimal Classification: 266.07
Subject Heading: MISSIONS ACTIVITIES
MISSION ACTION
FAMILY—RELIGIOUS LIFE

Scripture quotations marked NIV are taken from the HOLY BIBLE,
NEW INTERNATIONAL VERSION®. NIV®. Copyright©1973, 1978,
1984 by International Bible Society. Used by permission of Zonder-
van. All rights reserved.
    Scripture quotations marked The Message are taken from The
Message by Eugene H. Peterson. Copyright © 1993, 1994, 1995, 1996,
2000, 2001, 2002. Used by permission of NavPress Publishing Group.

Design by Janell E. Young
Cover design by Theresa Barnett and Bruce Watford

ISBN-10: 1-56309-967-5
ISBN-13: 978-1-56309-967-0
W053124•0106•2.5M1

Contents

A Letter from the Author

Ever since I was given the opportunity to participate in a hands-on missions project, my life has never been the same. I'm not sure I can put into words what happened that day as I served in a Backyard Bible Club in a little town outside of Memphis, Tennessee. All I remember is thinking the experience was one I wanted to do over and over again. It was an amazing feeling to share the love of Christ by becoming Christ's hands and feet to children that were hungering for love and attention. This book is a compilation of ideas for missions projects for a family to do together. I pray that as you attempt them, you will also have that same feeling to wash over you.

I would like to express my heartfelt love and thanks to my wonderful husband, Steve Heartsill, who shared his thoughts, did research, helped me refine my crazy ideas, and encouraged me throughout this project. I would also like to thank the many missions leaders out there whose names I do not know who submitted missions ideas that were published through a bimonthly newsletter for missions leaders. You may notice some similarities of your ideas as you read through these pages. As my husband says, "There aren't many new ideas, they are just refined to fit the situation and the audience." I pray you will read through these ideas and tweak and refine them to fit your needs. I also pray that as you work together to share the good news of Jesus' love, you will be changed and challenged to become a missions advocate! Have fun!

—Tonya W. Heartsill

1

January: Missions Ideas for Cold, Winter Days

Family Missions Calendar. Along with a new year come many resolutions for everything from becoming more health conscious to learning to play the piano. This year, make a resolution to lead your family in becoming more missions-minded. How do you do that? Begin by printing a blank calendar from a computer. If you don't have a program on your home computer that prints calendars, purchase a blank calendar at a discount or office supply store. Plan a family get-together to determine what activities you would like to do as a family to remember missionaries and missions work that goes on around the world. You may decide to write something on each day of every month or you may only want to write something on each Saturday or Sunday. Once you determine how often you would like to do some type of family missions activity, begin brainstorming ideas. Your missions activities can be as simple as praying for a specific missionary on his or her birthday to surprising a family from a shelter and taking them out to get ice cream. Here are a few ideas to get you started:

- Donate children's books to a new church in your community.
- Give a fruit basket to an unchurched shut-in in your community.
- Write a thank-you note to your pastor.
- Offer to go grocery shopping for an unchurched senior adult.
- Make a bank out of a milk carton and save change for a special missions offering.
- Learn and practice using five new words in another language.
- Make cookies and take them to your teacher.
- Pray for a missionaries' kid (MK) who is celebrating his or her birthday.
- Visit residents in a nursing home.
- Invite an international family to dinner.

What Time Is It in . . .? It is easy to get caught up in your daily schedules of school, work, church, and whatever else is going on and forget about your promise to pray for the missionaries. Purchase a wall clock that strikes each hour and hang it in a prominent place in your home. Choose a special missionary family you know personally or a missionary family that has ties to your church and find out what time it is in the country where they serve. Set the clock according to the missionary's time. Write the name of each member of the missionary family on a piece of masking tape or a sticker. Stick each of the names on a certain hour of the day. For instance, at 12:00, stick the name of the family; at 3:00, stick the name of the mother; and at 6:00, stick the name of the father, etc. As the clock strikes each hour, encourage your family to pray for the missionary. Not only will your family be reminded to pray, they will also learn about the time differences around the world. Choose a different missionary family each month and change the clock accordingly.

Winterize the House of a Senior Adult Neighbor.
Winter can be a hard time of year for senior adults who have problems with their health. It is important for their houses to be winterized so the winter weather stays out and the heat stays in! The process of winterizing a house is fairly easy. Several simple steps that only cost pennies and take a few minutes can make a world of difference to the heating bill. Begin by choosing an unchurched senior adult you would like your family to serve. Contact the individual and ask if your family can get his or her home ready for winter. Once you have permission, purchase the needed supplies for the project. You may want to visit the house before the service day to determine the needs of the individual. Purchase weather stripping, insulation for pipes, and plastic sheathing for the windows. Choose a day when the whole family can participate in the project. Spend the day cleaning out gutters,

raking leaves, covering windows with plastic, and installing weather stripping around doors and windows. End the day with a cup of hot chocolate and spending time with your new senior adult friend.

Create a Missions Display. Do your church members know what type of missions projects they sponsor? If you are looking for ways to keep your church family in the missions information loop, consider setting up a permanent missions display table in a high-traffic area of the church. Set up a table and make a sign entitled "Missions in Our Church." Decorate the table once a month, highlighting the different missions endeavors of the church. Highlight missions trips by framing pictures from the trip and displaying various items bought on the trip. Bring attention to a particular social organization by putting out brochures and offering information on the ministry. Emphasize an unreached people group by putting a map of the world on the table with the country highlighted and displaying pictures and facts about the people group. Enlist someone with creative flair to change the display each month. Your attention to detail will help your church family understand what is going on in your missions ministry.

Blanket and Coat Collection. Although this idea isn't a new one, it is one that is very important to those that are in need during the winter. Lead your church or Sunday School class in collecting new blankets and gently used or new coats for a local homeless shelter. Advertise your collection in the church bulletin. Publish the location of the collection site and a specific deadline for collecting items. Decorate several large cardboard boxes and clearly label them with appropriate signs. Allow the collection to continue for several weeks. Once all the coats and blankets are collected, sort through the items and make sure they are in good condition and clean. Fold the items neatly and pack in a box. Deliver the boxes to a local homeless or abuse shelter.

Chili Cook-off for Missions. There is nothing better than a hot cup of chili on a cold winter evening! Why not capitalize on this idea and challenge your church members to a chili cook-off for missions? Invite those who believe their chili recipe is the best to enter the contest. Challenge each entry to select a different church ministry or local ministry to highlight. They need to collect information (flyers, brochures, photos, etc.) about the ministry and create a table display that incorporates their chili entry. Choose several people from the church to serve as judges. As entries are brought to the church, assign each one a number so the judges won't know who made each pot of chili. Have the entries set up their table display and reserve one cup of chili for the judges to taste. Volunteers can serve the remaining chili to those who come to eat. Award small prizes for the following categories:

- Best Flavor
- Most Likely to Burn Your Mouth
- Most Unusual Taste
- Best Presentation

Once the winners have been selected and announced, take a few minutes to share the importance of missions in your church.

Snow Day Fun. Although a "snow day" from school is great for kids, it can be a real problem for parents who are expected to make it to work no matter what the weather is outside. Organize a neighborhood snow day of fun! Contact several stay-at-home parents in your church and ask them if they would be willing to volunteer to supervise during the event. Plan a special day of activities to be held on the next snow day. Hold the event at your church or neighborhood center. Pass the word around the community that your church will be holding a snow day event for children who need somewhere to go while their parents are at work. Plan to hold your event from 7:00 A.M. to 5:00 P.M. Make sure parents pack a lunch for their child. Plan to play games, watch movies, make a craft, and play in the snow! For a special treat, make snow cream. (Adjust the recipe accordingly.) The recipe follows:

SNOW CREAM

1 cup snow	**1 tablespoon sugar**
½ cup whipping cream	**2–3 drops vanilla**

Mix together and place in the freezer until it is time for the special treat!

Prepare a flyer to send home with each child. Include information about the church, its ministries, and the plan of salvation. Provide a phone number of someone to call if he or she is interested in knowing more about Christ or the church.

Coffee/Hot Chocolate Giveaway. During cold winter days it is always a treat to have a nice cup of something hot to warm your bones. Fill a thermos with hot coffee and/or hot chocolate. Load your family in the car along with your thermoses and plastic foam cups. Drive around the city and have your family look for people working outside. Ask them to look for people who are serving the community through their job, such as police officers, construction workers, sanitation workers, mail carriers, etc. Once you find someone who needs a nice hot cup of coffee or hot chocolate, stop and give that person his or her choice of hot beverage. As you give out the drink, be sure to tell the person you appreciate the work he or she does for your family and your community. If it is appropriate, invite the person to your church for worship.

Emergency Kits. Along with winter weather there is a threat of losing electricity in your home. Help your neighbors prepare for an emergency by presenting them with a simple emergency kit. Purchase large resealable bags and have your children pack them with the following items: a candle, matches, small flashlight, batteries, bottled water, and local utility and emergency phone numbers. Include a small note in the bag that lets the recipient know what church you represent and include the plan of salvation. Use this opportunity to teach your children the importance of preparing for emergencies. Discuss with them what to do if there should be an emergency situation at home. Walk around your neighborhood and present the bags to each family. If you don't know them, let them know who you are and the importance of having an emergency kit in their home.

Crafts for Shut-ins. Teach your children the importance of remembering those who live alone by planning a simple craft activity that can be made and given to someone who is in need of a visit. So many senior adults in our society live alone and have very few people who visit them on a regular basis. A simple gift and visit will mean the world to them.

Contact an unchurched senior adult or his or her caregiver for suggestions of what to make. Visit a local craft store to get ideas for simple crafts. Choose a craft that is age appropriate for your children. Take into consideration the person who will be receiving the craft. Does the person enjoy plants? Does the person love to cook? Is the person bedridden or have limited mobility? Consider having your children paint terra-cotta pots and plant a flower for the plant lover. Bake a loaf of banana nut bread or a peach cobbler and place it in a pretty basket for the food lover. Have your children write a story and draw pictures to make a storybook to share with someone bedridden. Whatever you do, choose a craft project you and your children can do together and be proud to present to anyone who may need a little pick-me-up!

2

February: Missions Ideas That Show Love

Cookie Ministry. In many churches new members have their hand shaken once and then they are on their own to find their niche in the church family. It can be hard to meet new people and get involved in churches where everyone knows everyone and most have been members since they were in diapers.

Plan to start a ministry to new members. Once someone joins your church, plan to drop by his or her home or work and deliver a batch of homemade cookies. During February, make heart-shaped cookies and wrap them in red tissue paper and place in a decorative bag or box for a dramatic presentation. Cut out several different sizes of heart shapes out of red and pink construction paper.

Using a silver gel pen, write on each heart one reason why you love your church's involvement in missions. For example, you could write, *We love our church because we are missions-minded. We love our church because we care about children. We love our church because we help the poor. We love our church because we teach English to non-English speakers.* Write facts about the church missions ministries that would be interesting to the family or individual who joined the church. Remember that a single person will be interested in different aspects of your church than a family with teenagers.

After delivering the batch of cookies, plan to follow up with the family or individual to answer any additional questions they may have about the ministries of the church.

Heart Your Pastor/Leader. During this month of love, why not tell your pastor or missions leaders thanks for preaching and teaching about missions and encouraging members to participate in missions activities? One way to do this is to "heart" their yard. Begin by purchasing several pieces of red and pink poster board. Cut the poster board into several large heart shapes. On each heart, use a permanent marker and write how your pastor/leader represents missions to the church members. Try to think of as many things as possible. The more hearts you have, the better. Once you have finished writing on the hearts, attach a paint stirrer (many home improvement and paint stores will give you these free) on the back of each heart with masking tape or duct tape. Once all the hearts are ready, drive to your pastor's or leader's home and stick the heart messages in the front yard. What a surprise your pastor/leader will have when leaving for work the next morning!

Flowers for the Forgotten. Sometimes even the simplest gesture can make someone's day move from humdrum to unforgettable. Go to your local grocery store or florist and purchase a bouquet of wildflowers. Look around your kitchen to find old glass bottles or jars to serve as vases for the flowers. Individual-size juice bottles work great! Clean the bottles thoroughly and tie a piece of ribbon or raffia around the mouth of each jar and fill with water. Divide the bouquet in half to create two small bouquets. Snip the ends of the flowers to fit in the vases you decorated. Arrange the flowers attractively in the vases.

Now comes the fun part. Think of unchurched people in your life you come in contact with every day, but don't know very well. This could be a day-care worker, mail carrier, grocery clerk, receptionist, or convenience store clerk. Whomever you choose, present the person with one of the flower bouquets. Place the bouquet in a place where the recipient will find it, yet not know who the giver is. Add a simple note to the bouquet to let the person know you appreciate the work he or she does and that you thanked God for the person and his or her work. Include a Scripture verse that directs the person's thoughts to Jesus.

Valentine Cards for Those Who Have Lost Loved Ones. Valentine's Day can be a hard day for those who have lost their longtime loves. Help them feel special by making homemade Valentine cards and delivering them to their doors with warm smiles and big hugs.

Start with an 8½-by-11 piece of cardstock. Fold the paper in half to make a card. Allow your children to decorate the front of the Valentine card using rubber stamps, construction paper, markers, paints, pictures from magazines, etc. Use whatever craft supplies you have around the house. Allow the children to be creative as they decorate the special card. Once the card is decorated, write a short poem, quote, or verse on the inside. Have your children sign the card with a personal note to the individual.

When Valentine's Day arrives, deliver the card to an unchurched individual. Invite the individual to a special lunch at a restaurant or in your home. Ask the individual to share stories about how he or she met his or her long-time love and why the person was so special. Your gift of love will mean more than you will ever know.

Lend a Helping Hand to a Single Parent. Being a single parent can be an overwhelming job. After working a full-time job and running here and there for everything from grocery shopping to T-ball practice, the single parent never seems to find time to do anything special for him- or herself. Choose an unchurched single parent in your neighborhood who would enjoy having a special day arranged by your family.

Begin by providing a full day of day care for the individual's children. Locate a responsible caretaker to take the children for an entire day. Once the children are taken care of, plan a special day for the single mom or dad that would allow him or her a chance to have some relaxation time. Consider taking the single mother for a manicure and pedicure and then out to dinner. The single father might enjoy a day at the movie theater or college basketball game. Talk with the individual about what he or she would like to do before you make plans. Chose activities the individual would enjoy doing. Once you make the plans, purchase gift certificates or tickets for whatever activities you have planned. If possible, purchase tickets or gift certificates for the individual and a guest. Don't impose your family on the person for an entire day. Allow the individual to choose whom he or she would like to spend the special day with. While the individual is gone to enjoy the day, plan for a team of friends to go into the individual's house and clean it from top to bottom. Get permission from the single parent beforehand. Some people may not feel comfortable having someone else come into their home without them being present. If the individual doesn't feel comfortable allowing you to clean his or her home, think of some other ways you could make his or her life easier. Consider doing yard work, cooking a week's worth of meals that can be put in the freezer, or doing any needed repair work around the house.

Once the single parent and his or her children return home, let them know your family will be available to lend a helping hand whenever possible.

Breakfast for a Stranger. Who can resist a hot cinnamon roll or sausage biscuit? Not me! Plan to show your love and appreciation for someone special by buying the person breakfast for no particular reason at all. Imagine the reaction you will receive when your family presents the tollbooth worker with a big breakfast purchased from your favorite fast-food restaurant as you pay your toll in the morning. Think of the appreciation your children will get when they present their school crossing guard with a warm blueberry muffin and cup of coffee on their way to homeroom. Attach a card with a Scripture that reflects Jesus' love for the individual. It only takes a minute to show someone you appreciate them and therefore make someone's day. It is amazing to see how God can take one small act of kindness to change someone's life for the better. Try it and see what happens!

Adopt a Nursing Home Resident. Living in a nursing home can be very lonely. Although family members promise to call and visit, many nursing home patients find themselves alone and unconnected from the outside world. Look in the phone book for nursing home facilities in your area. Contact the director and talk with him or her about what you would like to do. Once you have permission, ask some of the following questions:

- What is the name of a patient our family could visit and get to know?
- What personal items would the resident like to have in a gift basket?
- Are there special dietary needs to consider when bringing gifts to a resident?
- What day/time would be best to visit the resident?
- Would it be appropriate for children to visit the resident?

Once you know a little more about the resident, take your family shopping for a gift basket for the resident. Include some of the items the director mentioned in your conversation. Plan a time when your family can visit the resident. Before you go, prepare your children for the visit. Explain to them the condition of the resident you will be visiting and what to expect. When you visit, take the resident the gift basket and let him or her know you care. Spend time sharing with the resident some details about your family. Ask questions about the resident's family and his or her past. If possible, plan to visit the resident once a month.

Decorate a Hospital Waiting Room. Have you ever been in a hospital waiting room that was bright and cheery? Most hospitals provide some chairs and a phone; but other than that, waiting rooms can be very sterile. Plan to make Valentine's Day decorations with your children and decorate your local hospital waiting rooms. Before you get started, contact the hospital volunteer coordinator and discuss with him or her your idea about decorating a waiting room and get permission to move forward with your plan. Once you have permission, start making decorations. Ask your children to cut out large heart shapes from construction paper or poster board. Decorate the hearts with glitter and paint pens. Hang the hearts on the walls and from the ceiling. Add streamers and balloons around the room. Use your computer to make a large banner. Decorate a large basket and fill it with individually wrapped cookies, crackers, fruit, and candy. Put a note in the basket explaining who provided the items and inviting people to partake of anything in the basket. Write out several verses of comfort and cheer on index cards to include in the basket. When Valentine's Day is over, be sure to return to the hospital to remove the decorations and other items. Don't leave it for the hospital staff to clean up.

Showing Love for Missionaries. Many missionaries have sacrificed a lot to serve God. When a missionary family decides to answer the call to missions, they give up many comforts of home. Many move to places where there are no shopping malls, no movie theaters, and no restaurants to eat in every Saturday night. Contact your church staff to get the contact information of missionaries connected with your church. Contact one of the missionaries to learn about the family's needs and how to get items delivered to them. Take your family shopping to buy gifts for the missionary family. As you pack the box that will go to the missionary family, include a letter to the missionaries and a picture of your family. Your gift of love will be a wonderful surprise for a missionary family that greatly deserves to know they are not forgotten.

3

March: Missions Ideas That Will Give You a Spring in Your Step

Missions at the Gym. Along with the excitement that spring is just around the corner comes a feeling of dread with the thought of having to put on a bathing suit in a couple of months! It is this feeling that motivates us to return to the gym after a long winter break. If you and your family have a gym membership, plan a missions project that will minister to those who work out at the gym. Since most people who frequent the gym are trying to get in shape, consider handing out bottled water, energy bars, or power drinks to them as well as to the staff. Attach an index card, sticker, or tag to each item you give away. Include on the tag a verse that relates to strength or power. Also include information about the church you attend and the times of the services. As you give away the item, invite people to your church to find out more about the strength you have in Jesus.

Psalm 68:35 (NIV): "You are awesome, O God, in your sanctuary; the God of Israel gives **power** and strength to his people. Praise be to God!"

Exodus 15:2 (The Message): "GOD is my **strength**, GOD is my song, and, yes! GOD is my salvation. This is the kind of God I have and I'm telling the world! This is the God of my father—I'm spreading the news far and wide!"

Colossians 1:11 (The Message): "We pray that you'll have the **strength** to stick it out over the long haul—not the grim **strength** of gritting your teeth but the glory-**strength** God gives. It is **strength** that endures the unendurable and spills over into joy."

Little Bags of Blessings. If you live in a town that has a major highway anywhere near it, you will most likely come in contact with people sitting or standing on the side of the road with a sign with words to the effect of *Will Work for Food*. One way to provide for people in need is to give them a little bag of blessings. OK, so the title is a bit cheesy, but the idea is a good one. Begin by buying a box of gallon-size resealable bags. Sit down with your family and discuss what types of things someone might need if he was down on his luck and home-less. Use this opportunity to explain to your children that helping someone in need is what Jesus would do. Make a list of items that would be useful to someone who is homeless. Make sure the items you list are nonperishable and small enough to fit in the plastic bag. Consider items such as crackers, bottled water, travel-size soap and deodorant, candy, socks, and quarters. Take the entire family shopping to buy the items you will put in the bag. Check out your local dollar store for some cost-efficient items. Have your children decorate the resealable bags with Bible verses using permanent markers. Once the bags are stuffed, pack them in the trunk of your car. Whenever you come across someone who needs a help-ing hand, give him a bag and let him know you care.

Pass On the Passion. Easter is the perfect time to invite friends and family over to celebrate the life and death of Jesus. Include guests who are not Christians to celebrate the day with you and your family. Invite a family you have been praying for to join your family for an Easter celebration. Plan some special activities for the children such as decorating Easter eggs or an egg hunt. Serve a traditional Easter dinner and bake a special dessert. Before the meal, say a prayer and ask each person at the table to share his or her favorite Easter memory. Before your guests leave, present them with the *Jesus* video. Ask them to take some time to watch the video. Let them know you would like to get together with them again after they watch the movie to discuss the movie and answer any questions they may have about the contents.

Easter Basket Giveaway. When you think of Easter, you can't help but think of Easter baskets, chocolate bunnies, and jelly beans. Unfortunately, there are many children who don't get Easter baskets. Take your children shopping for candy and small gifts to fill Easter baskets for underprivileged children. Purchase small baskets and plastic eggs at area yard sales or at your local discount store. Let the children use permanent markers or stickers to decorate the plastic eggs with pictures of flowers, rabbits, and butterflies. Add a couple of decorated eggs to each basket. Fill the rest of the basket with candy and small gifts such as art supplies and toys. Include a note that tells the story of Jesus and why Easter is important. Allow your children to deliver the baskets to a children's home or women's shelter.

Remembering Annie Tea Party. Each year around Easter, Women on Mission® groups around the country discuss ways to encourage giving to the Annie Armstrong Easter Offering® for North American Missions. Plan a tea party for the mothers and daughters in your church. Encourage each woman who participates in the event to dress in a nice dress and wear a special hat to the celebration. Ask participants to bring a teacup and saucer to the event to serve as their admission. As guests arrive, have volunteers collect the cups and saucers and set them around the tables. Once the cups and saucers are set out, serve hot tea and homemade scones. (Following are a couple of recipes to get you started.) As the women are enjoying their tea, invite a woman in your church or association to share the story of Annie Armstrong with the group. If possible, invite a missionary to speak about her work on the missions field. Close the event in prayer.

CINNAMON WALNUT SCONES

3½ cups flour
½ cup walnuts, finely
   chopped
3 tablespoons sugar
1½ tablespoon baking
   powder
1 teaspoon salt

1 teaspoon cinnamon
½ cup cold butter or
   margarine
4 eggs
⅔ cup whipping cream
½ cup buttermilk

Combine the flour, walnuts, sugar, baking powder, salt, and cinnamon in a mixing bowl. Cut in the butter until the mixture resembles coarse crumbs. Combine eggs and cream in a small bowl and then stir into dry ingredients just until moistened. Turn the mixture onto a floured surface. Gently pat the dough into a 7-inch circle, ¾-inch thick. Cut the dough into 8 wedges. Separate wedges and place on a lightly greased baking sheet. Brush the tops of the scones with buttermilk and sprinkle with a sugar/cinnamon mix. Let rest 15 minutes.

   Bake at 450°F for 14 to 16 minutes or until golden brown.

STRAWBERRY SCONES

2 cups flour PLUS
½ cup flour for kneading
    dough
2 teaspoons baking pow-
    der
½ cup sugar

4 tablespoons butter,
    chilled
¾ cup milk or cream
½ cup chopped fresh
    strawberries

Mix flour, baking powder, and sugar in a mixing bowl. Cut in butter with a pastry blender. Stir in milk and strawberries until blended. Put dough on floured surface and gently knead into a ball. Flatten to 1½-inch thickness. Slice the dough in half and then into quarters or thirds and put on cookie sheet or stone. Bake at 400°F for 15 to 20 minutes.

Icing: Mix 1 cup powdered sugar and 1 to 2 teaspoons strawberry syrup. Drizzle over the scones when they are hot. Cool.

Coins for Annie. Are you wondering how to get your entire church family involved in giving toward the Annie Armstrong Easter Offering®? One way is to give out coin wrappers to every member of the church and challenge them to fill them for missions! Hand out quarter wrappers to adults, dime wrappers to college and high school students, nickel wrappers to elementary students, and penny wrappers to kindergartners and preschool children. Ask parents to talk with their children about why we are collecting money for the Annie Armstrong Easter Offering. Encourage Sunday School leaders to include information about North American missions during the

WE CAN DO THAT!

month of March. Allow families to collect their change throughout the month of the offering and ask them to bring in their filled wrappers on the last Sunday of the offering. Post the coin totals for everyone to see and celebrate as soon as the amount is totaled.

Family to Family. Get the name and contact information for a North American or international missionary from your state Baptist convention office. Contact that missionary and ask for the name and contact information of another family the missionary ministers to. Begin writing that family. Encourage your children to write to the children of this family and share information about their life.

4

April: Missions Ideas for Rainy Days

International Missionary Place Mats. If you are looking for a way to share information about missionaries around the world with your faith family, why not make missionary place mats to use during your Wednesday night dinner? Begin by finding out what missionaries have ties to your church. If your church doesn't have ties to a missionary family, check out Prayer Patterns in *Missions Mosaic* for specific names and assignments of missionaries. Once you have several names, do more research about the country and people group the missionaries serve. Ask your children to help you decorate 8½-by-17 pieces of cardstock with the information you find. Include the missionary's name and place of service on the cardstock. Include facts about the country where the missionary serves such as population, primary religion, job assignment, climate, etc. As you decorate the place mats, use bright colors to grab people's attention. Once you have decorated several place mats with missionary information, make appropriate number of color copies. If possible, laminate the place mats so they can be used more than once. Be sure to direct people's attention to the place mats and the information printed on them.

MK Birthday in a Box. If you want to make a missionaries' kid (MK) feel very special on her birthday, put together a birthday party in a box that can be mailed to the child for her special day. Contact your state WMU office for dates of MK birthdays. Contact the MK's parents to learn about the MK's needs and likes and how to send the items. Take your family shopping for a birthday party that can be packed in a box. Purchase a boxed cake mix and frosting. Include cupcake liners and birthday candles in the box. Talk with your children about what makes a birthday special. Give your children a budget and let them purchase a present for the MK. Remember the present may be packed in a box and will have a long ride to its destination. Don't mail anything breakable or too heavy. Once your box is packed, cut up construction paper to make confetti and sprinkle it throughout the box. Put some balloons in the box and top it off with a special birthday card letting the MK know you will be praying for her or him on her or his birthday. Be sure to send the box early so it will reach its destination close to the MK's actual birthday. Be sure to mark the MK's birthday on your calendar and lead your family in a special time of prayer for the child on the special day.

Sunshine Bags. Does your family know an unchurched person who could use a little bit of sunshine in his life? Maybe it is someone who is facing another chemotherapy treatment or someone who has recently lost a loved one. Or, you may know someone who has lost his job or is getting divorced and needs something good to happen to him. A sunshine bag may do the trick! A sunshine bag is a bag filled with goodies that will make someone smile. It can be a paper bag filled with homemade chocolate chip cookies or a resealable bag loaded with little trinkets. If you are handy with a needle and thread, you might want to make small fabric bags and fill them with little gifts. Whatever you decide to fill your bag with, make sure you include some Scripture verses appropriate for the situation the recipient is experiencing. To find verses of comfort, cheer, or encouragement, check out a concordance. For online passage lookup, go to www.gospelcom.net. Choose several verses that would be inspiring for the recipient and type them on your computer. Add a border and clip art to make a personalized card. If possible, add a New Testament Bible to the bag. Mark all the Scripture verses relating to comfort or encouragement with a highlighter. Sunshine bags can be filled with just about anything; just take into consideration that the object is to make someone smile.

Following are directions for a simple drawstring bag that can be made out of a large felt circle.

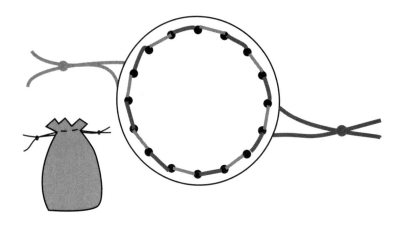

Cut a large circle out of brightly colored felt, using a pro-
tractor or a dinner plate as a template to make sure your
circle is symmetrical. Once you have cut your circle out,
make a series of holes or slits between ¼ to 1¼ inches
from the edge of the entire circle. (The neck of the bag
is formed by threading a cord through these.) If you
have access to a leather punch, use that to punch per-
fect-sized holes; otherwise, cut the holes with small
sharp-pointed scissors.

Cut two pieces of cord or ribbon long enough to
thread through the holes. Thread one of the cords
.through each of the holes and knot the ends together.
Take the other cord and thread through the holes in the
opposite direction and knot the ends together. When finished, the knots for each cord should be on opposite
sides of the bag. When you pull the cords in opposite
directions they will gather the fabric together to form the
neck of the bag.

(Adapted from http://www.hiraeth.com/ytg/projects/bags/bag1.htm)

Missionary Photo Album. Do you have a hard time bringing missions into your daily life? With one or two other family members, make a missionary photo album to help make missions real to your family. Begin by collecting missions magazines, such as *Missions Mosaic, The Mag, Discovery,* or *GA World,* that publish pictures of missionaries. Cut out the pictures and paste them in a photo album. Do research online (use other resources also) about each of the countries or states where the missionaries serve. Include information in the photo album about the countries or states. Draw simple maps of the areas and mark with a red star the cities where the missionaries serve. Include interesting facts about the countries or states. What kinds of food do they eat? What kinds of jobs do the missionaries have? What languages do they speak? Include decorative background papers and stickers that can be found in craft stores or discount department stores to embellish your photo album. Once the photo album is complete, place it where your family can use it during your family prayertime. As your family prays, look through the album and remember to pray specifically for the missionaries and the work they are doing. If possible, correspond with the missionaries in your photo album to get up-to-date information to add to your photo album. Before you know it, it will feel like the missionaries you are praying for are part of the family!

Have Crafts, Will Travel. Do you have crayons, markers, construction paper, glue, scissors, and yarn hidden in various drawers and containers in your house? Do you find yourself saving paper towel rolls, empty baby food jars, and old magazines just because you may need them one day? If you are guilty of any of the above, your family is probably a great candidate for making a traveling craft box. Begin by purchasing a large tackle box or toolbox. Choose a box with multiple containers/trays where you can store many different sizes of craft items. Go through all your craft supplies and discard anything that is old or doesn't work anymore. Group all similar objects together. Organize items such as markers, crayons, scissors, glue, and beads in individual resealable bags. Place construction paper, tracing paper, and watercolor paper in a shirt box or manila envelope. After all your craft supplies are organized, pack your craft box with a variety of the craft items. Now that your box is ready, do some research online (use other resources also) for easy-to-make craft projects for kids. Choose craft items that can be made from the supplies you have in your box. Try to find craft projects that would be appropriate for several age groups. Once your box is ready and you have a couple of crafts you can make, take your box on the road! Visit a children's hospital wing, go to a picnic pavilion at a popular park, or invite neighborhood kids to come to your garage for a few hours of making cool crafts. Wherever you decide to go with your craft box, be sure to share the gospel story as the children work. You may be surprised at how God will use your traveling craft box!

Cut Coupons for a Single Parent. Being a single parent can bring about many challenges. Growing children with a constant need for nourishment can be one of the greatest! As you look through the newspaper, in home magazines, and online, collect coupons to give to an unchurched single parent. Have your children help you cut the coupons and organize them in different categories such as food, personal items, cleaning supplies, restaurants, etc. Purchase a small coupon organizer at your local discount store. Set up different tabs in the organizer to file coupons appropriately. Call local grocery stores and ask if they offer double coupons. Include a list of these stores in the coupon organizer. Take your children shopping for staple foods that are needed in any pantry. Include items such as sugar, flour, bread, cereal, etc. Allow your children to choose a special item to include in the bag. Deliver the groceries to the single parent in your community, along with the coupon organizer. Tell the single parent you appreciate him or her and the hard work he or she does each day. Offer to babysit sometime in the future.

Email Pals. Remember the days when kids had pen pals? It was so exciting to get a letter in the mail from someone who lived in another part of the world! Introduce your children to missions by setting up communication with a missionaries' kid (MK) who lives in another part of the world. Contact your state Woman's Missionary Union® office to find the contact information of an MK from your state. Have your children write an email to the child, letting the child know who they are and about their hobbies and interests. Have your children ask questions about the MK and where he or she lives. If possible, include a picture of your children by scanning a picture and attaching it to the email. Send update emails to the MK once a week to let him or her know your family is praying for him or her and the work his or her family is doing.

5

May: Missions Ideas to Show We Care

Invite a Missions Volunteer to Dinner. Participating in a missions trip across the US or across the world can be a life changing event. Many times people come home from a missions trip and they give a short testimony in a worship service and that is the last we hear of their adventure. One way to bring missions into your home is to invite people who have been on a missions trip into your home for a meal. Whether it is a college student who has participated in summer missions or a single adult who has given up his or her vacation time to serve overseas, every person who has been on a missions trip has a story to tell. Not only will your family have an opportunity to learn about missions firsthand, they will also become acquainted with someone who is excited about missions. What a great role model a young adult who loves missions can be for your children! To make the event even more fun for your family, plan a menu that would feature a special dish from the country where the missionary served. If they went to Mexico, plan a simple meal of chips, salsa, and tacos. If they went to India, look online (use other resources also) for authentic Indian recipes. Check out the ingredients and determine which recipes would be suitable for your family. You might just want to serve a dessert from the region if the cuisine would not be appetizing to your family. Ask your guest to bring pictures of his or her trip for the whole family to enjoy. Before the individual arrives, locate on a map the state or country where the person served so your family will be somewhat familiar with the area. Have your children prepare some simple questions to ask about the trip. If possible, invite another family from your church who may not be involved in missions.

Gift Cards for Missionary Wives. As missionaries return to the States for stateside assignment, they immediately begin to think about the things they can get in the States that they can't get in the country where they serve. Simple items such as peanut butter, powdered soft drink mix, and candy bars that we take for granted can become luxuries to a missionary serving overseas. Instead of trying to purchase items you think the missionaries might want, allow the missionaries to choose the items themselves by presenting the missionary wives with gift cards to discount stores. Most discount stores offer gift cards in amounts ranging from $10 to $100. A gift card will allow the missionaries the freedom to purchase whatever items they need. Obviously they know exactly what they need and how much room they have to pack the items for shipping to the country where they serve. Your thoughtfulness will be greatly appreciated as they walk the aisles of the store and choose the items that are most practical and most needed for their ministry.

Share the Gift of Reading. Imagine what it would be like if you didn't have books, magazines, and newspapers to read in your language. What if every newsstand, bookstore, and magazine cart carried items in a language you couldn't read. That is what missionaries experience every day as they serve in other countries. Although missionaries spend countless days learning the native language of the people they minister to, there is always a sense of relief to see something printed in their native language. Choose a missionary family that would enjoy a special package filled with reading material. Contact the missionary family to learn what they enjoy reading and how to send the reading material. Take your family to a Christian bookstore or look online at www.wmustore.com to purchase a book that would be appropriate for each member of the missionary family. Consider best-selling inspirational books for the parents, teenagers, and children. Once you have purchased each family member a book, purchase a missions magazine for each family member. Consider sending a copy of *Missions Mosaic* to the mother, *Missions Leader*ᴸᴹ to the father, and the appropriate children's magazine to the children to read. As you pack the box to be shipped, include special bookmarks that your children make for each member of the missionary family. Your gift of reading will definitely be a smash hit with a family needing a small reminder of home.

Missions Closet. We have all heard of a clothes closet or a food pantry, but what about a missions closet? The closet can be used to collect items that would be useful for missionaries visiting on their stateside assignments. The missions closet would store practical items such as toiletry items, food staples, and basic everyday necessities. As you decide what items to collect, think about a missionary family that is returning to the US for stateside assignment. What items do you think they would have to leave behind? Although many missionary houses provide the basic items such as linens, towels, cooking items, etc., there are still many everyday items that would have to be left behind. Put together a list of items your church family can collect for the missions closet. Publish the list in the church bulletin and let church members know what you will be doing with the items and where the items will be collected. Once you start the missions closet, let your associational office know of your new ministry. Ask them to keep you informed of missionaries who will be living in your area. As a missionary couple visits, allow them to take whatever items they need from the missions closet.

Missionaries' Kid Speaker. As missionary families return home for stateside assignment, their children come with them for the visit. Consider inviting a missionaries' kid (MK) to speak to children's and youth groups at your church. Their point of view will be much more exciting to the children and youth than that of an adult missionary. Ask the MK to begin by telling a little bit about his or her life on the missions field. Ask the MK to explain about the cultural differences and the customs of the region. Allow a time for questions and answers. Allow the children/youth from your church to ask questions about the MK's life overseas. What is school like? What do you do for fun? What do you plan to do when you graduate from high school? What is your favorite food? After the meeting, plan a time of fellowship so the youth in your church will feel comfortable getting to know the MK on a personal level.

Adopt an Unreached People Group. Teach your family about missions by adopting an unreached people group to learn about and pray for daily. Begin by introducing the idea to your family during a family Bible study time. Discuss with your family what region of the world they would like to learn more about. After you have decided on a country or continent, visit www.peoplegroups.org to find out more about the unreached people groups in that particular area. Spend some time reading through the names and information published on the people groups Web site. After you have read through each of the names, have your family spend time in prayer, asking God to guide you as you choose a specific people group to pray for each day. Once you choose one of the people groups, continue to do research to find out more information on the region where the group lives, their culture, and lifestyle. Take time before meals with your family to pray specifically for the people and for those who will answer the call to missions and share the gospel in that specific area of the world.

Praying for Missionaries. Many times it is hard to know how to pray for the missionaries. Although praying "God bless the missionaries" is a good place to start, teach your family to pray more specifically for missionaries by using some key thoughts and phrases. Here are a few to get your family started:

- Pray the missionaries will have healthy relationships with the nationals they work with each day.
- Pray the missionaries learn the language and become fluent quickly.
- Pray for the missionaries' relationships with area churches and religious leaders of the region.
- Pray the missionaries will use their time wisely.
- Pray the missionaries will have boldness to witness whenever God gives them the opportunity to do so.
- Pray for knowledge of the people and their customs.
- Pray for energy for the missionaries when they feel drained.
- Pray for healthy marriage/family relationships.
- Pray for the missionary family's extended family that must learn to live with their children and grandchildren being overseas.
- Pray for creativity as the missionaries come up with new ways to present the gospel message to the nationals in an understandable way.
- Pray for safety and health.

Tell the Missionary Story. One of the best ways to minister to a missionary family is to tell their story to those back home. One way to do this is through a quarterly newsletter. If you have a computer and like to write, it is easy to put together a simple newsletter to distribute to area churches so they can learn more about the missionaries they support through the Cooperative Program, the Lottie Moon Christmas Offering®, and the Annie Armstrong Easter Offering®. Newsletters allow missionaries to share specific stories about how God is moving as well as give up-to-date prayer requests. Begin by establishing a relationship with a missionary family that is currently serving on the missions field. Let the missionary family know you want to share their story with your church family and area churches. Ask them to send you emails periodically about the work they are doing on the field. Collect the information and once a quarter compile it into a simple newsletter format. If possible, include recent photos of the missionary family and specific information about each member of the family. Include information that would be interesting to read. Share interesting facts about the country where the family serves such as customs, recipes, and games the children play in the region. Instead of printing the newsletter and mailing it to church members, start a missions ministry email list for those families that would like to learn more about missionaries and the work they do on the field.

Send Off a Missionary. Do you have a college student in your church who has decided to do missions work for a summer, semester, or two years? If so, throw him or her a "missionary shower." Many college students live with garage sale finds and hand-me-down furniture. Send the student off in style by hosting a shower. Contact the student or his or family and ask what the student needs. Ask your church family to bring a gift that would help a student missionary set up a household. Practical gifts include dishes, silverware, towels, sheets, kitchen utensils, cookware, and gift cards to discount stores. Plan a time of fellowship and sharing during the shower. Allow the student missionary to share some details about the work he or she will be doing on the missions field. Ask those who come to the shower to commit to pray for the student missionary while he or she is away from home. Serve some simple refreshments and end the evening by having the student missionary open his or her gifts to show everyone what he or she received.

6

June: Missions Ideas for Reaching Your Community

Baby Bottle Banks. Do you have a crisis pregnancy center in your community? If not, do you know someone who is pregnant who could use a helping hand during her pregnancy? Maybe it is an unwed mother struggling to make ends meet. Or maybe it is a mother dealing with a high-risk pregnancy. One way to minister to the needs of these women is through a baby bottle ministry in your church or community. Begin by purchasing baby bottles at a dollar store or discount department store. Pass the bottles out to your Sunday School class, WMU® group, children's group, or to your entire church congregation. Ask families to collect their daily leftover change in the bottles. Set a specified amount of time for collecting money and then ask everyone to bring the filled bottles back to the church on a specific date. Count the change and convert it into bills. Present the cash to the pregnancy center or to a mother in need. Allow the mother to use the money in whatever way that would most benefit her and her child. If you don't feel comfortable giving the cash directly to an individual, give gift cards or purchase items that are most practical for a new mother.

Birthday Cake Block Party. If you are looking for a new twist on the old idea of a neighborhood block party, consider hosting a neighborhood birthday cake block party. By celebrating everyone in the neighborhood's special day, you will get to know your neighbors better as well as enjoy a piece of birthday cake!

For this special block party, begin by finding an appropriate location for the party. If your weather is fairly dependable in the summer, plan to hold the block party in a community park or in the front yards of several homes in a central location of the neighborhood. If weather is unpredictable, plan to hold the event in a community meeting place or commons area. If no such place is available, set up a few tents to provide some shelter in case of rain.

Once your location is determined, secure several volunteers in your church to make birthday cakes. You will need one cake to represent each month of the year. Ask the volunteers to decorate the cakes according to what month they are assigned. For example, for July birthdays you could decorate the cake with a patriotic theme or for an October cake you could decorate with pumpkins.

Once all your cakes are taken care of, invite the neighborhood to attend a birthday party. Send out invitations to each family in the neighborhood. Be sure to include time, date, and location of the event on the invitation. Determine how you will decorate your location. Hang streamers and blow up balloons. Invite a clown to come and make balloon animals for the children. Invite someone to play the guitar and sing songs during the event. Ask your church puppet team to perform. Have an area where guests can make crazy hats. Basically, plan a birthday party for the whole family to enjoy.

Once your birthday party participants show up, ask them to visit the table that has the cake for their birthday month. As they are given a piece of cake, have volunteers stationed at each of the cake tables to talk with guests about their spiritual birthdays. Use the opportunity to share the love of Christ and how they can have a spiritual birthday as well as an earthly birthday.

Father's Day Community Art Show. Every neighborhood has people known to be closet artists. They are the ones who love to paint, draw, mold, and create something out of nothing. Many are just waiting for a chance to share their work with others. Why not give them that chance?

Plan an art show at your church. Put out the word that you are looking for area artists to create an art piece that relates to Father's Day. Set a date when all the artists must turn in their art pieces for display. Ask for volunteers in your church to make small appetizers for the event. Print a simple program that gives information about each of the artists participating in the art show. Secure volunteers to greet guests at the entrance of the church to give out programs and direct people to the art show.

Display the art pieces around the room on walls and on tables. Make a placard for each piece with the name of the piece and the artist printed on it. Play soothing instrumental music in the background. Choose one art piece to give away through a drawing. Invite the artists to mill around during the show to talk with people who come to the show. Be sure to invite visitors to come to your church in the future.

Emergency Bags for Fire Victims. Imagine what it would feel like to wake up and realize your house is on fire. The confusion and devastation of the moment would cause even the most level-headed to rush from the house without even the most basic necessities. One way your family can minister to the immediate needs of those who have lost everything they own in a house fire is to prepare resealable bags with essential items and give them to families in need. Purchase large gallon-size resealable bags. Fill each bag with the following items: a razor, travel-size shave gel, shampoo, toothpaste, soap, adult-size toothbrush, lotion, deodorant, tissues, washcloth, brush, and Bible. Include a brochure about your church. Take the bags to your local fire department for distribution to those who experience a house fire.

Help for a Nonprofit. One way you can minister to the needs of others is by donating your time and talents to a nonprofit organization. Many nonprofit organizations need volunteers to do everything from office work to sorting donated items. Many of the jobs they need done can easily be done by family members of all ages. Begin by looking in your phone book for a nonprofit organization in your area. Contact the organization and ask if they need volunteers. Tell the ages of your children and ask if they have any jobs that would be appropriate for children to do. If nothing else, ask if you can pick up trash or plant flowers around the facility. Plan a day when your entire family can go to the organization to volunteer. Take the opportunity to teach your children the importance of volunteering.

Welcome Basket for New Neighbors. If you have new neighbors, show them some hospitality by presenting them with a Welcome to the Neighborhood basket. Purchase inexpensive baskets of various sizes and shapes at yard sales or discount stores. When a new family moves to the neighborhood, fill the basket with homemade goodies, a map of the area, important emergency phone numbers, and information about your church and the ministries it offers to families. Top off the basket with a bouquet of wildflowers. After the family gets settled into their new house, plan a time when your whole family can go over and meet the new neighbors. Present the basket and introduce your family. Offer to be a contact for the new neighbors if they have any questions.

If filling a basket with homemade goodies sounds like an impossible task, call your local pizza parlor and order a pizza. Ask the pizza parlor to deliver the pizza to your home. Deliver the pizza to your neighbors and personally welcome them to the neighborhood. Be sure to give the family your name and contact information if they should have any questions about the neighborhood. Invite them to visit your church on the next Sunday.

Teach a Class. Do you feel you have knowledge on a subject that you would like to share, yet don't have an outlet to do so? Why not organize a community study night? Consult friends and neighbors in the community to find experts in the areas of child rearing, finances, marriage, home improvement, cooking, crafts, etc. Classes could be offered one night or one night a week for several weeks. Once you have your teachers and classes lined up, secure a location for the classes. If your church agrees to get involved, secure several rooms in the church to accommodate the different topics that will be taught. Advertise throughout the community the classes you plan to offer. Print up flyers that include class descriptions and the names of the teachers. Post an announcement in your local post office and community center. Let people know the classes are free (unless you have to charge a small amount for materials used during the class) and everyone is welcome to attend. Consider offering classes for teens and children so the whole family will have a class to go to on your community study night.

WE CAN DO THAT!

7

July: Missions Ideas for Hot Summer Days

Honor Those Who Serve Our Country. The Fourth of July brings about thoughts of those who have given their lives so we can enjoy freedom: freedom to worship however we wish; freedom to have our own opinions about issues; and freedom to express those opinions. Honor those in your church and community who serve in the military, police department, fire department, and first response teams by hosting an old-fashioned Fourth of July barbeque. Ask the men of your church to do the barbequing and ask the women to make potato salad and apple pies. Have the children make many thank-you cards to be given to the guests of honor. If your church doesn't have an area to hold a community picnic, reserve an area at a local park where you can hold such an event. Print special invitations to send to those in your area who currently serve, who have previously served their country in the military, or who serve their community as police officers, firefighters, or first response teams. For entertainment, hold an old-fashioned three-legged race and a game of softball. End the afternoon with a time of devotion and sharing to express gratitude for those who have given up so much for the cause of freedom. Have the children give their thank-you cards to each military and emergency response personnel.

Give Away a Cold Drink. On hot July days, when the sun is beating down and sweat threatens to pour down your face the minute you walk out the door, there isn't anything better than a nice, cold beverage to quench your thirst. Fill a cooler with ice, soft drinks, and water. Load your family in the car and drive around your community to look for people who are working in their gardens, mowing their lawns, doing construction work, or exercising. As you come upon someone working outside, offer a cold drink. As you give out drinks, let the person know what church you are from and invite the person to visit. You may be surprised how God will use the gift of a simple soft drink to someone who is tired and thirsty from a hard day's work.

Share Your Garden. By July, the garden is bursting with ripe tomatoes, squash, cucumbers, green beans, and corn. If you don't intend to can the vegetables for a long winter ahead, look for friends and neighbors who would

WE CAN DO THAT!

appreciate receiving some of the excess. Instead of loading up the vegetables in a plastic bag, spruce up your offering by washing the vegetables and presenting them in a fruit basket with a big bow on the front. Choose some of your favorite vegetable recipes, such as salsa, squash casserole, or cucumber salad, and type the ingredients and directions out on the computer. Include the recipes with the vegetables in the basket. Consider giving the basket to an unchurched family, a new neighbor, a single mom, an elderly friend, or a family you would like to invite to your church.

Party with a Purpose. Are you one of those people who can't resist a good party? If so, consider giving a party that has a special purpose of sharing the good news of Christ. Begin by purchasing the book *Party with a Purpose* by Page Hughes (New Hope® Publishers). Read through the book and determine the type of party appropriate for those you would like to invite. The book gives ideas for parties appropriate for anytime to specific holiday and seasonal parties. Each party idea includes a theme, decoration ideas, refreshment ideas, and a devotional that goes with the theme. Some of the parties featured include a princess party, checkered flag party, a patriotic picnic, and a hurricane party. Before you know it, you will be considered the party queen and people will be asking you if they can come!

Garage Sale for Missions. As the old saying goes, "One man's junk is another man's treasure." Spend a few days having your family go through old toys, clothes, household goods, and closets to find items that can be sold in a yard sale for missions. Encourage your family to get rid of anything they have not played with, used, or worn in the last year. Use the opportunity to explain to your children the importance of donating items to charity. Explain how you will use the money made from the yard sale to help someone do missions work.

Advertise your yard sale in the classified section of your local newspaper. Price the items you want to get rid of at very reasonable prices. Display like items together in such a way that they are easy to see and easily accessible for inspection. Make large signs with arrows and the address of your yard sale location. Post the signs on major roads that lead to your location. Once your yard sale has been going for a while and all the hot ticket items are gone, consider offering anything left for a quarter. Donate whatever items that are left to the Salvation Army or local thrift store.

Once the sale is over, decide with your family where the money will go. Do you want to donate it to a special offering? Is there a youth or college student in your church who is going on a missions trip? Is there a missionary your family knows who would be able to use the money to further the gospel? Once the family agrees on where the money will go, present the money to the individual or organization and offer your prayer support as they share the gospel message.

Water Days at the Park. After the kids have gone to camp and been to all the Vacation Bible Schools in the area, they tend to get a little restless. Plan a special water day event to cool them down and occupy their time for an afternoon. Let your children spread the word around the neighborhood that you will be hosting a day of water games at the church. Enlist other adults to help you with the event. Ask all participants to wear their bathing suit and bring a towel to the event. Load up a large plastic container with water balloons for a water balloon toss. Plan relay races that use buckets of water. Set up a slip and slide by using plastic tarps and a water hose, or purchase some simple water sprinkler toys at your local discount store and let the kids run through the sprinklers. Serve large hunks of watermelon as a snack and have a wet and wild time! At the end of the event, share a Bible story with the children.

Here are a few water game ideas to get you started:

Disk Douser Relay. Lay out a relay course on a flat, grassy area. Mark a starting point with a rope and place a chair 100 feet in front of the starting line. Set up four buckets of water, two on either side of the course. Place six sponges in each bucket. Have the kids form teams of four. One team will be the "dousers" while the other team will line up behind the starting line. Give each player behind the starting line a flying disk to wear on the top of the head. On "Go," the first player behind the starting line will make his way to the chair on the other end of the course. The object is for the player to circle the chair and make his way back to the starting line. As the player tries to do this, the dousers will throw wet sponges at him with the intention of knocking the flying disk off his head. The douser team will receive two points for every flying disk knocked off. The team that is racing will get two points for every team member who makes it back to the starting point with the flying disk still on his head. Switch team once all four members run the relay. The runners will then become the dousers. Play until everyone is soaked!

(Adapted from Michael, Warden, ed., *Great Group Games for Youth Ministry* [Loveland, CO: Group Publishing, Inc., 1994], 76.)

Waterline Sneak. Divide the kids into three teams. Ask the first two teams to line up facing each other with about four feet between them. Have them put on a blindfold and then give them a glass of water. The third team will then take their towels and put them on their heads like a turban. The object will be for members of the third team to pass through the waterline without getting their turbans wet. They can move through the two lines however they wish, but they must remain on their feet. As they move through the line, the members of the first and second teams will try to douse them with their cups of water as they pass. Continue to rotate through the teams so that each team has a chance to go through the waterline. The team with the driest towels wins!

(Adapted from Michael, Warden, ed., *Great Group Games for Youth Ministry* [Loveland, CO: Group Publishing, Inc., 1994], 93.)

Minister to Vacationers. If you live in or near a vacation destination, develop a tourist guide to help visitors know where to eat, what to do, and how to get to certain tourist destinations in your area. Begin by designing an attractive cover for your tourist guide. Develop a theme that you will use throughout the booklet. If your town is known for its beautiful beaches, use a beach theme. If it hosts a summer peach festival, take your camera out to the peach orchard and take some snapshots of kids picking peaches. Scan the pictures into your computer and insert them onto your cover page. Be creative as you design your cover so it will grab the attention of tourists. Once your cover is designed, plan what information to include inside. Consider including a restaurant guide with addresses, phone numbers, and hours of operation. Include a list of local attractions along with brief descriptions, directions, cost, and hours of operation. Include information about local hospitals and emergency numbers for visitors to use while vacationing in your town. On the last page, include information about your church and include an invitation for the visitors to worship with you on Sunday. Don't forget to include the plan of salvation. Distribute the booklets to area hotels, welcome centers, and rest stops.

Prayer for Hurting People. Every year many believers around the world are being punished because they believe in Jesus. There are also believers hurt during natural disasters reported in the media. As your family learns of persecuted believers or natural disasters, find that location on a map. Pray for the affected in these areas and that more people will learn of Jesus.

.

Encouragement Notes for Missions Trip Teams.
These days most churches participate in several missions trips. Contact the church office to get the names of team members for an upcoming trip and select one member. As a family, write individual or separate notes to that member. Let the member know he or she will be prayed for and share a favorite Scripture. Deliver to the team member just before he or she leaves for the trip.

76

8

August: Missions Ideas That Focus on School and Students

Family-to-Family School Supply Collection. There are children around the world who dread the first day of school because they aren't able to walk into their new classroom with a new backpack or new crayons. These children are those whose families can't afford to buy the necessary school supplies for the new school term. Imagine the smile your family can put on a child in need's face when you present him or her with a new backpack jammed with new tablets, pencils, crayons, markers, and glue! Begin a school supply collection in your church for needy children in your community. Ask your church family to donate new backpacks, notebooks, pens, pencils, crayons, markers, glue, and scissors. Set up a large collection box in the lobby. Decorate the box with brightly colored paper and label it clearly. Ask your church if it can provide a new pair of shoes and jeans in addition to the school supplies. Work with your area schools to know who needs school supplies and the types of supplies needed. Either donate the items directly to the local board of education, or take the items directly to the children in need.

Feed the Teachers. Honor the teachers at your children's school by preparing a meal for them during in-service days before school begins. Gather together several parents who would be willing to help you prepare and serve breakfast or lunch to the teachers. Plan your menu and divide the work between the volunteers. Get the children of the volunteers to make muffins or cookies, depending on which meal you choose to serve. Talk with the school principal to plan a day and time when you can serve the meal. Decorate the eating area with a festive back-to-school theme. Set up a serving line and allow the teachers to serve themselves. Have servers give out drinks and pour refills throughout the meal. Take time during the meal to thank the teachers for all the work they do throughout the year to provide a good education for your children. Give each teacher a daily devotional book dedicated to teachers. Let them know you will commit to pray for them each day.

Library Book Drive. As a new school year approaches, plan a book drive to collect books for schools around the nation that lack needed resources. Contact your state WMU office or the associational office for a school in their area that lacks resources. Put a small ad in your local newspaper, to let your community know about your book drive. Print flyers to post on front doors of houses so everyone in the community will get involved. Let people know what day you will be in the neighborhood to collect the books. Plan to have several collection areas around the neighborhood so it will be convenient for people to drop off their books. Consider collecting books at the post office, grocery store, church, and school. Once all the books are collected, work with your local librarian to sort and catalog the books in the library system. Ask a family to volunteer to personally deliver the books.

Devotional Book for Teachers. Being a teacher can be very stressful. Teachers constantly worry about everything from keeping their students' test scores high to making sure students are safe from the time they arrive at school to the time they leave. Help your children's teachers cope with the stresses of their jobs by compiling a devotional book for them to use each day before their class arrives. Begin by working with your children to write a week's worth of devotionals. Ask each family member to choose an appropriate Scripture verse that deals with subjects teachers face each day. Ask them to keep each devotional at 200 to 300 words so teachers will be able to read the devotional before their day begins. Encourage them to share personal stories and examples in their writing. Set a deadline for the devotionals to be turned in for editing and compilation. Also, have your children create covers for the booklet. Once the devotionals are completed, print them as a booklet and add a cover. Include a letter on the first page that lets teachers know they are appreciated. As you give out the devotional booklets, invite the teachers to visit your church.

Adopt an International Student. Many international college students leave the US with their degree but without the experience of visiting in an American home. Imagine traveling overseas to live for several months and never experiencing what family life is all about. Give an international student a special gift by inviting him or her into your home to experience American life. Prepare a traditional meal indigenous to your area. If you live in the South, prepare fried chicken. If you live in the North, prepare a large batch of steamy clam chowder. You get the idea. Choose a menu that may be new to your guest's taste buds. After dinner, share some of your family photos with your guest. Show him or her around your home and allow him or her to ask questions about your family traditions. Continue to cultivate a relationship with the student. Invite the student to share special holidays with your family. Send the student encouraging notes when he or she is facing finals. Prepare a care package for the student when he or is studying for a big test. As you get to know the student, invite him or her to experience worship with your family. Introduce the student to other college students in your church. Pray that

God will give you the opportunity to share your faith with the student before he or she returns home.

Volunteer for a Teacher. Teachers can always use an extra pair of hands to grade papers, tutor students, or prepare for a special lesson plan. Contact a school in your community and ask how your family can volunteer. Let the principal know when you are available to volunteer in the classroom. Talk with the principal about what you would like to do. Do you feel comfortable enough in a particular subject area that you could tutor a child that has fallen behind? Are you a gifted artist who can design and implement an interactive bulletin board? Whatever you like to do, there is a place in the local classroom for you. As your family volunteers, be a positive example to the teacher and the other students in the class. Shine Christ's love through every word and action you do. If the opportunity arises, share the reason behind your positive attitude.

Honor the Behind-the-Scenes Workers. It takes a lot of people to make a school run smoothly. Of course you have the principal and the teachers, but how often do we show appreciation for the secretaries, cafeteria workers, and janitors? Take time to serve those who constantly serve others by having your family make appreciation cards. Purchase construction paper and markers. Encourage your family to write short messages to show their appreciation for those who serve in the office, cafeteria, and cleaning their classrooms. Present each of the workers with the card and personally tell each worker how much you appreciate his or her service.

What Is in the Missionary's Backpack? If you have the opportunity to share information about a missionary with a group of children, consider discussing with them what a missionary would have in his or her backpack if he or she were going overseas.

To begin this game, stuff a backpack with the following items: passport, vaccination certificate, malaria tablets (or an empty prescription bottle), mosquito net, driver's license, toilet paper, Bible, towel, soap, matches, map of country, water filter, cup, plate, eating utensils, candle, medical kit, hat, screwdriver, nails and screws, rope, sewing kit, radio, and money. If you do not have all of the items, improvise with a similar item or substitute something else that represents the same idea.

Once you start the lesson, ask the children to name some things they would take with them if they were going on a missions trip. If you have a chalkboard close by, list the items on the chalkboard. Once the children have called out several items, explain that you have a missionary's backpack with you and you want to show them what is inside. Take the items out of the backpack one at a time and place on the floor. Name each item as you pull it out of the backpack, but don't go into any detail about any of the items. Once you have all the items out of the backpack, cover them with a sheet or towel.

Give each child a piece of paper and ask the children to list as many of the items in the backpack as they can remember. Allow the children to work on their lists for 1 minute. After 1 minute, lift up the sheet and allow the children to look at the items for 30 additional seconds.

82

Give the children another 2 minutes to complete their lists. When the time is up, have the children switch papers with a friend to check their answers.

Call out each item and allow the children a few moments to check the lists. Award those with the most correct answers with a small prize. Once you have a winner, go back and describe the importance of each of the items in the missionary backpack. Allow the children to ask questions about the items. Close the session with prayer for the missionaries who serve in remote areas of the world.

Mentor a Teen. In today's society there are many teenagers in your church family who are faced with tremendous peer pressure and heartbreaking family issues. If you have teenagers of your own, it is likely these teens come into your home on a regular basis. Take time to let teenaged guests in your home know you care about them. Whenever your teen brings a friend home, make a point to get to know the friend. Offer to make a special meal for the friend or, better yet, ask him or her to help you prepare a special meal. Take time to listen to his or her stories and ask pertinent questions about his or her interests and hobbies. Play a game of basketball with the friend or help him or her with a scrapbooking project. If the teen comes from a single parent home, offer to help the parent by carpooling to events or practices. If the teen is not a Christian, take time to pray with your teenager for the salvation of his or her friend. Pray specifically for opportunities for your teen to share Christ with his or her friends.

Chocolate Chip Cookie Giveaway. Do you remember what it was like to be a college student? A meal usually consisted of ramen noodles and a diet soft drink! Grab the attention of college students on your community campus by offering students free home-baked chocolate chip cookies. Contact campus authorities to get proper permission to be on campus. Plan a special giveaway at your local campus to commemorate the delicious cookie that has stolen our hearts. Gather together several families to make chocolate chip cookies. Set a time for families to make and pack chocolate chip cookies. Put the cookies in a resealable bag along with an encouraging Scripture verse and information about the opportunities your church offers to college students. Fill a large basket with the cookies and go to the college campus student center.

Feed the Hungry. As your family sits down to a meal, discuss the fact that there are people in your community and around the world who have little or nothing to eat. Discuss ways your family can help.

- Collect food for a food bank.
- Serve a meal at a soup kitchen.
- Give money to a world hunger fund.

9

September: Missions Ideas That Give a World Perspective

Collect Eyeglasses for the Needy. Imagine what it would be like day in and day out to not be able to see clearly. Now, imagine what it would be like if you couldn't see clearly and you couldn't read or write because of it. There are people all over the world who live without clear vision because they don't have the money or resources to buy glasses. Consider starting a used eyeglass drive at your church to help those around the world who need eyeglasses. Partner with Medical Ministry International (MMI) to provide donated eyeglasses and frames to people in Central or South

America, Eastern Europe, or Southeast Asia. Once you and your family collect the eyeglasses and send them to MMI, they wash, sort, and make any needed repairs to the donated glasses. They use a computer to determine the prescription of each pair of glasses. The glasses are then assembled into groups and sent out to people in need. To download an eyeglass collection kit and also find out more information about this project, visit www.mmint.org. Recycle joy and help people around the world through medical missions!

Operation Christmas Child. I'm sure you have heard of it, but now is the time to get your church family involved with this great outreach to children around the world! Operation Christmas Child is a ministry of Samaritan's Purse. The project allows those who participate to get involved with a hands-on missions project by purchasing small gifts that will be packed in a shoe box and shipped overseas to children who may not receive any gifts for Christmas. In every shoe box, a gospel tract in the child's language is included so each child who receives a box will also receive the gospel message. To begin, find an empty shoe box with a lid. Wrap the box and lid separately with colorful Christmas wrapping paper. Decide whether you will purchase a gift for a girl or a boy and then choose one of the following age categories: 2–4, 5–9, or 10–14. Now comes the fun part, take your family shopping for a variety of small gifts to fill the box. Consider purchasing age-appropriate small toys, school supplies, hygiene products, or other practical items such as T-shirts, socks, jewelry, candy, etc. Once your box is packed, go to www.samaritanspurse.org to download and fill out the appropriate form to include in your box and also get directions on where to send your gift. Whether you send 1 box or 1,000 to Samaritan's Purse, there will be a child somewhere in the world who will have a special Christmas because of you.

Shoes for Orphan Souls. Don't you love getting a new pair of shoes?! Share that exciting feeling with orphaned children around the world who have never had a new pair of shoes by partnering with Buckner Orphan Care International to collect new shoes to be distributed to needy children around the world. The project is simple and very easy to get started. Begin by publicizing in your church the collection date for new children's shoes. Make large posters to put up around the church to let your church family know when and what you are collecting. Run announcements in your church bulletin and on the church's Web site or newsletter. Ask for volunteers to help you to sort the shoes once they are donated. On the collection day, collect and sort the shoes according to size. Once the shoes are sorted, pack them in boxes and ship them to Buckner's warehouse in Dallas, Texas, for distribution. It is that easy! For specific information and further directions on what to do and where to send the shoes, visit www.shoesfororphan souls.org.

Get a Kick Out of Sharing. Help give a child who lives in a Third-World country back his or her childhood by joining World Vision in their Get a Kick Out of Sharing soccer ball collection drive. This program was set up with the intent to distribute new and gently used soccer balls to needy children around the world. By distributing soccer balls, World Vision hopes to give children the opportunity to play, have fun, and remember what it means to be a kid. The program asks for groups to donate soccer balls and small hand pumps to the World Vision organization for distribution around the world. For more information on how you can lend a hand to this project, visit www.worldvision.org and click on Donate Soccerballs on the left-hand side of the screen. Send your donated, deflated balls and small pumps to: World Vision Gifts-in-Kind, Distribution Center, Soccer Ball Program, 210 Overlook Drive, Sewickley, PA 15143.

People Group Prayerwalk. One way to help your church family become more aware of missions around the world is to set up a people group prayerwalk down the hallways of your church. Begin by doing your homework. Go online and look up information about unreached people groups around the world. Check out www.joshuaproject.net or www.imb.org for statistics, pictures, and specific information about people groups around the world who have not heard the gospel message. Choose several people groups to focus on during your prayerwalk. Make a large poster for each of the people groups. Include a picture that represents the people group, statistics about the location of the world where they live, and specific things participants can pray about during the walk. Hang the posters along a long hallway or in several different rooms where families can gather comfortably. On index cards write numbers 1 through however many posters that you made. Once families arrive, let them know they will be participating in a prayerwalk for unreached people groups around the world. Explain the definition of an unreached people group to the families (a people group among which there is no indigenous community of believing Christians with adequate numbers and resources to evangelize this people group). Read the following Scripture verse: "'This gospel of the kingdom will be preached in the whole world as a testimony to all the nations, and then the end will come'" (Matt. 24:14 NIV). Give each family an index card that will tell them where to begin on the prayerwalk. Allow each family 5 minutes at each poster. Ring a bell to let the families know when to move to the next station. After 30 minutes, bring all the families back together and end the activity with a group prayer.

Experience Babel. Have you ever tried to imagine what it must have been like at the Tower of Babel when one minute you could easily understand what everyone was saying and the next you couldn't? Language barriers are one of the main reasons we haven't been able to successfully communicate the gospel message to all peoples of the world. Give your family a taste of "Babel" by leading them in a simulation where they have to create a language of their own and then teach it to other family members. The outcome will be a great representation of what our missionaries face every day. Begin by reading Genesis 11:1–8. Ask the family to discuss how the people must have felt during this time in Scripture. Divide your family into adults and children. Ask each of the groups to create a brand-new language. Tell them their language must be different from English and it must include both action words and descriptive words. Each of the languages they create must include the following:

- A greeting or welcome
- A description of something (an old man)
- A phrase that asks a question (Where is the restroom?)
- A good-bye greeting

Give each group 10 minutes to come up with their words and phrases. Once time is called, pair two groups together and give them 5 minutes each to teach the other group their four words/phrases. Explain that the groups can only teach by using their new language. They can not use English or pig Latin! Once the simulation is over, ask the following discussion questions:

- Were you able to teach your language to your partner?
- How did you go about teaching your partner group your language? Where did you start the process?
- How did it feel to be the one teaching? The one trying to learn?
- How important is it to communicate with others?
- How can we relate this experience to missionaries who serve around the world?

Close by explaining there are over 6,000 distinct languages that are spoken around the world today. Some missionaries must commit to first learn the language, then figure out how to write it. After that has been accomplished, the gospel message has to be translated

92

into the appropriate language. The process is often a long one. Lead your family in prayer for the missionaries who serve in remote areas where there is no written language.

(Adapted from an idea in *Bright Ideas!* [Orlando, FL: Wycliffe Bible Translators, 1997]; www.wycliffe.org.)

Around-the-World Tea Party. Are you looking for a way to welcome new women into your missions group? You can easily start the tradition of holding a mother-daughter tea party that features tea from around the world. Once a month, find a mother-daughter team in your church family who would be willing to host a tea party in their home for the new women and their daughters who have been visiting or have joined your church. Begin by purchasing several different types of tea for the participants to taste (check out specialty coffee shops for a variety of teas). Once you have decided on the tea flavors, look for missionaries who serve in the area of the world where the tea is grown. For instance, if you are serving Chai tea, be prepared to share information about people who live in India where drinking Chai tea is an afternoon tradition. As you prepare for the tea party, look for and purchase inexpensive teacups at yard sales or thrift stores. Wrap the teacups in decorative bags along with a personalized invitation to the tea party. Give a teacup to each of the women and their daughters in your church who are new or have visited recently. Ask each participant to bring her teacup with her to the tea party. As you sample the various teas from around the world, share information about missions work going on in that region. Before moving on to taste the next tea, pray for the missionaries who serve in that country. For some added fun, ask participants to wear their favorite hats to the tea party. For information on different teas from around the world check out www.planetroasters.com. Click on Facts for information about coffee and teas around the world.

10

October: Missions Ideas for Cool Autumn Days

Missions Involvement Appreciation Month. Plan a special date night for church members who have been on a missions trip. Invite one of them and their family into your home for a meal and time of sharing. Ask him or her to bring items he or she purchased on the trip to talk about. They might also bring a few pictures to share over the meal or afterwards. Have all the children present listen for things about the place being discussed. How can they use this information to learn about the world in which they live?

Adopt a Police Officer. Show your appreciation and support for the police officers and their supervisors by adopting a police officer for a month. Begin by contacting your local police department to find out how many officers work in your community precinct. Let the police supervisor know of your plans and ask for the name of one of the officers. Once you have a name, commit to pray for, encourage, and show gratitude to that officer for a month. Send notes of encouragement, provide the officer with small gifts (such as baked goods or devotional books), and pray diligently for the safety of the officer as he or she protects your community. Ask if there are specific prayer requests that the officer might have that your family can pray about for him or her. At the end of the month, have a special meal delivered to the precinct to let the officer know how much you appreciate him or her and the work he or she does for the community. This can also apply to fire departments, EMTs, and military personnel.

A Moving Ministry. What do you think the number one anxiety is when moving to a new town or state? Meeting new friends! Start a "moving" ministry in your church to offer assistance to families moving into your area. By helping families unload their furniture and other belongings into their new homes, your church can become the first contact they have with the community. Begin by finding a core group of families for the ministry. Ask for volunteers with trucks and trailers to get on board with your idea. Once you have a core group of five to seven families, advertise your services at your community post office, truck rental company, and realty companies. If you have realtors in your church family, ask them to

98

help promote the ministry with families that are planning to move to the community. Print up flyers with the contact phone number of the ministry. Post the flyers around the community and share your ministry idea with the church family. Before you know it, you may have more work than you can handle. Your ministry will give your family the opportunity to share Christ's love with those who may not know Him. Before you finish with the new family, be sure to give them information about your church and the different ministries offered. Follow up with the family after they get settled. Let them know you care about them by presenting them with a welcome basket.

Change a Battery, Save a Life. Each year, thousands of homes across the United States experience the devastation of a house fire. Help your neighbors take precautions against house fires by reminding them to check the smoke detectors in their homes. Begin by finding families who would be willing to go door to door to ask residents if they have checked their smoke detectors in the last year. Provide each household with a 9-volt battery so they can change the battery in their smoke detector. If the resident will allow you to come into his or her home, change the battery for the resident. Make sure each volunteer wears a name tag that clearly identifies his or her name and the church he or she represents when going door-to-door. Volunteers will need to visit in groups of two or three. Make sure that a male and female visit together. If the resident is not at home, prepare a door hanger that gives the name of your church and the reason you are leaving a

9-volt battery! Be sure to provide information about your church at each home.

Tour-Around-the-World Progressive Dinner. When the weather turns cool and the days grow shorter, plan a progressive dinner that focuses on missions and missions work that is being done around the world. Begin by finding four or five families in your church that have been on missions trips to various parts of the world or those who grew up or lived in a different country. Ask them if they would be willing to open up their homes for a progressive dinner and share about their experiences while on mission. Assign each family to prepare a portion of the meal (appetizer, salad, main course, dessert) from recipes from the country they are representing. If they don't know where to find these recipes, look online (and in other resources) for ideas. Ask the families to plan a short presentation about the country they visited. Explain that each stop on the tour should include photos and music from the country they are representing. The host family will also need to plan to share information about their trip and the people they encountered. Once you have finished the assigned course, close the visit with prayer for the missionaries who serve in the region represented. Continue to the next stop on the tour!

Pumpkin Harvest Festival. With Halloween right around the corner, churches are always looking for alternatives to the holiday that seems to celebrate more bad than good. Consider hosting a pumpkin harvest festival.

Plan a community family celebration and incorporate some of the following activities to make your event fun for the whole family. Pass out a flyer about your church and its ministries. Include the plan of salvation.

- *Pumpkin seed spitting contest.* Toast pumpkin seeds in the oven and then see how far competitors can spit the seeds.
- *Bible verse pumpkin carving contest.* Ask each Sunday School class to carve words into pumpkins to make Bible verses. Each pumpkin will have a different word carved into it. Once the pumpkins are lined up correctly, you can read the Bible verse.
- *Pumpkin pie eating contest.* Find several contestants who love pumpkin pie and have them compete against each other to see who can eat the most pumpkin pies in one minute!
- *Pumpkin launch.* See who can toss a pumpkin the farthest. Be sure you have plenty of pumpkins for tossing!
- *Pumpkin "hide-and-seek."* Find several different sizes of pumpkins and paint a point value on each one according to its size. For a small pumpkin, paint the number 5 on it with acrylic paint; for a medium-size pumpkin, paint a 10, etc. Hide the various sizes of pumpkins around the festival area. Have competitors find as many pumpkins as they can. The person with the highest point value will win a small prize.
- *Square dance.* End the evening with an old-fashioned square dance. Check around your community to see if there are square dancers who can help you with teaching the dances and calling out the moves during the

dance. Plan to hold the dance in the church parking lot. Put out bales of hay for participants to sit on.

FamilyFEST. How fun would it be to participate in a family missions experience? Check out www.wmu.com/getinvolved/ministry/volunteer to learn about FamilyFEST℠. Each year there are several locations to choose from. Start saving money to participate in one of these life-changing experiences.

Scriptures at Halloween. If your family lives in an area where children still trick-or-treat door-to-door, try getting Scriptures to the children. Buy candy that is big enough to hold a stick-on file folder label. Print verses on the labels that are simple enough for a child to understand. Place the labels on the candy.

11

November: Missions Ideas That Show Your Thanks

Helping New Moms. Celebrate new life by knitting or quilting baby blankets for young mothers who contact teen pregnancy centers. Begin by contacting a center that promotes Christian values and learn how many blankets they would need. Find families in your church who can knit or quilt baby blankets. For children who don't know how to make blankets, this is a great opportunity for them to learn. For more information on how to knit a baby blanket, search online or check out how-to books at your local library. When the blankets are completed, attach a special prayer, Scripture verse, or the plan of salvation to each blanket and present the blankets to the center.

Make a Point to Say Thanks. As you reflect on the past year and think about all you have to be thankful for, take time to list the people in your life who have blessed you throughout the year. Make a list of all the people in your life that you are thankful for. Don't forget to include the mail carrier, the kid who walks your dog, your Sunday School teacher, and your neighbor who waters your plants when you are away on vacation. Once you have your list made, draw a line down the middle of your paper and begin to list one thing you can do for each person on your list to let each one know he or she is a blessing to you. Your act of kindness doesn't need to cost a lot. It can be as simple as sending notes of appreciation or an invitation to a Saturday morning brunch. Consider some of the following ideas as you determine how you will show your thanks for those who have blessed you throughout the year.

- Put a love note in your spouse's or child's lunchbox.
- Wash your neighbor's car.
- Have a pizza delivered to someone's door.
- Treat someone to a movie and buy the popcorn!
- Pick a bouquet of flowers and deliver them.
- Offer to wash someone's windows.
- Put a chocolate kiss on your child's pillow.
- Pull weeds in a neighbor's yard.
- Give a compliment.
- Treat someone to lunch.

WE CAN DO THAT!

Celebrate a Bizarre Holiday. There are countless bizarre holidays that are on the calendar every month. If you are feeling a little crazy and want to make someone smile, plan to celebrate a crazy day. You may get a strange look or two, but you will more than likely make someone's day. Here are a few of the bizarre holidays that are celebrated in the month of November.

- November 1: National Author's Day. Purchase a book by your favorite author and give it away to someone.
- November 7: Hug a Bear Day. Purchase a teddy bear to give to a child or to a policeman to give away to a child who is experiencing trauma.
- November 17: Take a Hike Day. Take your children for a hike in the woods. Play a game of "I spy" as you hike.
- November 21: World Hello Day—Learn how to say hello in at least five different languages. Try out your new vocabulary on your co-workers.
- November 23: National Cashew Day. Buy a tin of cashews and walk around the office and offer them to your co-workers.

A Month of Missions and Giving Thanks. Are you looking for ways to help your family be reminded of missions and to give thanks? Create a November calendar on your computer and write one way to do ministry and to give thanks for each day of the month. Add some cute clip art and make copies for each member of your family. Encourage families to follow the suggestions written on the calendar. A sample calendar follows.

Sunday	Monday	Tuesday
1 Write a note of encouragement to a co-worker or friend.	**2** Take breakfast to your child's bus driver or crossing guard.	**3** Make a fall wreath for your neighbor's door.
8 Put up a bulletin board in your church that promotes missions.	**9** Rake your neighbor's leaves.	**10** Offer to do the dishes after dinner to give your mom a break.
15 Take one of the ministers at church to lunch.	**16** Offer to babysit for a friend with small children so he or she can have a night off.	**17** Call your grandparents.
22 Give your pastor a popular book for his library.	**23** Take your spouse's car to be cleaned professionally.	**24** Invite an international student to share Thanksgiving with your family.
29 Help a senior adult decorate his or her house for Christmas.	**30** Make a gingerbread house with your kids.	

November

WE CAN DO THAT!

Wednesday	Thursday	Friday	Saturday
4 Send an email to a long lost friend.	**5** Buy some flavored coffee to make at the office for everyone to enjoy.	**6** Bake an apple or pumpkin pie for your Sunday School teacher.	**7** Count the number of TVs in your home. Give $5 for each TV to missions.
11 Put a special note in a loved one's lunchbox.	**12** Take the neighborhood kids to the pumpkin patch to pick out a pumpkin.	**13** Send an ecard to a missionary. Let him or her know you are praying for him or her.	**14** Bake a batch of muffins to deliver to the nearest college dorm.
18 Invite a single adult to share a homemade dinner with your family.	**19** Clean out the gutters of a senior adult's home.	**20** Leave a candy bar in your mailbox for your mail carrier. Include a note of thanks for all he or she does.	**21** Write encouraging notes for a loved one on self-stick removable notes and put them up all around the house.
25 Take Thanksgiving lunch to a shut-in.	**26** Ask a senior adult if he or she would like to go Christmas shopping with you.	**27** Buy a special Christmas ornament for your hair dresser.	**28** Bake a cake for your WMU director.

Celebrate the Veterans. We often forget to thank those who serve our country in the armed forces. Take time to show them their service is appreciated by honoring them on Veteran's Day. Plan a special time of recognition in your Sunday service for all those who have served in the armed forces in the past, as well as those who are currently serving or have loved ones serving. Ask all the veterans to stand up for recognition. Allow each one who stands to share where he or she served. Include a time of testimony from a veteran. Ask a veteran to share how God helped him or her through a difficult time during his or her tour of duty. Present each veteran with a small gift to let him or her know his or her service and dedication to the safety of the country is appreciated. Serve a potluck lunch and make the veterans in the church special guests. Set up a special table of honor for the veterans and their families to sit and enjoy lunch.

The Art of Giving Thanks. Although it is important to teach your children to say please and thank you, it is also important to teach your children the significance of giving thanks for what they have been given. In today's throwaway society, many children don't understand the meaning of giving thanks. During the month of November emphasize the importance of giving thanks by preparing a "thanks giving" box. Decorate a box using brown paper and a plaid orange bow. Add a few fall leaves to the top to make the box look special. On the top of the box write, *We give thanks for* . . . As family members think of something they are thankful for, put an

110

item like what they have named into the box. When the box is full, give the box to another family that is in need.

Secret Sponsors. If you haven't noticed lately, teenagers are attracted to relationships. They are more interested in who is going to be at an event than what they will be learning. Start a ministry to the teenagers in your church called Secret Sponsors. Ask families to commit to sponsor a teenager for the month of November. With their commitment, they will promise to support their teens by praying for them, sending them notes of encouragement, and surprising them occasionally with a Christian book or CD. The families will commit to encourage the students in their Christian walk. At the end of the month, hold a banquet for the teens and their family sponsors. Reveal each teen's secret sponsor during the banquet. Have them sit together during the banquet to get to know one another better. Ask them to conclude the evening by praying for one another. (This idea can also be done for a longer length of time. Consider having secret sponsors throughout the school year or through an entire year. If you do choose a longer time period, be sure to remind your families to do something for their assigned student several times a month.)

Thanks a Million. As you begin to gear up for ways to promote the Lottie Moon Christmas Offering® for International Missions, challenge your church family to give a million pennies to missions. Ask each Sunday School class to decorate a container to keep in their classroom to collect the change. Encourage families to wrap the pennies in coin wrappers before they are donated so it will be easy to count the pennies. Provide additional penny wrappers each week for families to take home and bring back full the following week. Each week as the penny wrappers are dropped into the decorated container, ask givers to think of a country, a people group, or the name of a missionary. Ask them to say a brief prayer that the money will help to spread the gospel. Make a display in the lobby of your church so the church family can see how the Thanks a Million campaign is progressing. Once your goal is reached, make an oversized check made out for $10,000 (or the amount given) to the Lottie Moon Christmas Offering. Place the check in a location of the church where everyone will see the results of the offering.

Serve a Servant. Every city has people in it who give of themselves day after day to those in need. Whether it is a social worker, a homeless shelter director, or a counselor at an abuse shelter, they dedicate their lives to serving others who have fallen upon hard times. Often these people go unnoticed and unappreciated for the service they provide. Honor someone who serves in a social organization by showering the recipient with small gifts of books, CDs, homemade goods, and gift certificates. Your outpouring of thanks will surely revive the recipient and let him or her know his or her work is appreciated.

112

12

December: Missions Ideas to Celebrate the Season

Lottie's China. This year promote the Lottie Moon Christmas Offering® for International Missions to your family by planning an evening with a Chinese flair. Decorate with Chinese lanterns, brightly colored materials, and pictures of the people and places of China. Set place settings around the table and put a pair of chopsticks at each place setting. Plan a menu beginning with an appetizer of egg drop soup. Serve a main dish of Mongolian beef, egg rolls, and rice. (If you don't feel confident preparing the meal, have it catered by a local Chinese restaurant.) Complete the meal with homemade fortune cookies. Inside of each fortune cookie, place a slip of paper with the name of an international missionary. Ask each family member to commit to pray during the month of December for the missionary whose name (and the people they minister to) is in his or her fortune cookie. For entertainment, share information about China and the missionaries who serve in China or share Lottie's story in a first-person narrative. Ask family members to pray about what they will give to the Lottie Moon Christmas Offering goal.

FORTUNE COOKIES

1 egg white
⅛ teaspoon vanilla extract
1 pinch salt

¼ cup unbleached all-purpose flour
¼ cup white sugar

1. Write fortunes on strips of paper about 4 inches long and ½ inch wide.
2. Preheat oven to 400°F.
3. Grease a cookie sheet with a thin coat of butter.
4. Mix the egg white and vanilla until foamy but not stiff.
5. Sift the flour, salt, and sugar, and blend into the egg white mixture.
6. Put teaspoonfuls of the batter about 4 inches apart on the cookie sheet. With the back of a spoon, smooth the batter into round shapes, making sure the batter is as even as possible. Don't make too many at first—these cookies have to be hot in order to form them. When they cool off, it's too late! Start with about 6, to see how many you can do.
7. Bake the cookies for 5 minutes or until they look golden on the edges (the middles normally look pretty pale). Prepare more cookies on another buttered cookie sheet while the first batch is baking!

8. When you take them out of the oven, use a wide spatula to put the cookies upside down on a wooden board. Quickly put the fortune in the middle of the cookie and fold the cookie in half. Fold cookie in half one more time, then place folded cookies into a muffin tin to cool.

Trim a Tree for Missions. If you are a missions leader in a small church or if you want to have a missions project for the children in your church to do during the holiday season, consider a mitten tree. Set up an artificial tree in a visible area of the church. Cut out an oversized mitten shape from construction paper or cardboard. On the mitten, write the words *Mittens for Missions.* Attach the "mitten" to the top of the tree in place of the traditional star. Place an announcement in the church bulletin that you will be collecting new sets of mittens to give to a homeless shelter during the holiday season. Clip clothespins all over the tree so people can clip the mittens they bring directly to the tree. You may want to put a few pairs of mittens on the tree at the beginning of the project as an example and a reminder of the missions project. Your church family will quickly see the results of their missions project as the tree is decorated with mittens of all shapes, colors, and sizes! Just before Christmas, deliver the mittens to a local ministry or homeless shelter.

Build a Gingerbread House. One way to build community among church members is to hold an international gingerbread house competition. Begin by advertising your event in the church bulletin. Encourage families to enter a house into the contest. Stipulate that all houses must be made from scratch by the families. If you want to make it more challenging, give each family certain requirements that must be met when building their house. For example, stipulate that each house must have a front door, at least three windows, and reflect a country, people group, or international missionary's work. Appoint a panel of judges to determine which gingerbread houses will receive a prize. Create crazy categories such as Most Creative Use of Candy, Most Likely to Fall Over Before the Competition Is Over, Best Decorated, Most International, etc., for the judges to use when determining prize winners. Award the prizes and then allow spectators to mill around to see each of the works of art and to take pictures.

Create an International Chrismon Tree. As the first Sunday of Advent approaches, consider decorating your church Christmas tree with chrismon ornaments. Chrismon ornaments are symbols or monograms that represent the different names of Christ. Each symbol represents a name taken from Christian history that reveals the nature and character of Who Jesus is. Originated in the Lutheran Church, this Christmas tradition teaches church members the true meaning of Christmas. Consider buying chrismon ornaments from WorldCrafts at www.WorldCraftsVillage.com. Search the Web site for other international tree ornaments and learn about the artisans who craft these ornaments. On every Sunday evening, have one family member hang an ornament on

118

the tree. Ask each family member to explain the symbolism of the ornament as he or she places it on the tree or tell about the artisan who made the ornament. Pray for the people who made each ornament and that the artisans will learn about Christ as they make new ornaments.

Give Away a Poinsettia. Poinsettias have always been a beautiful reminder that Christmas is right around the corner. Instead of purchasing poinsettias in honor or memory of someone, ask your congregation to purchase a poinsettia to give away to a shut-in, a nursing home resident, a single parent, a new family in town, or even a stranger. Contact local florists to see if discounts are available for large purchases. Once you find a florist who gives you the best deal, plan to purchase enough plants so that each family in the congregation can give a poinsettia to someone they want to show love to during the season. Set aside a special day for each family to come to the church to pick up a plant and deliver it to someone who is unchurched. Ask each family to deliver their plant and then meet back at the church for hot chocolate and snacks. As the families come back to the church, ask them to share any special stories that resulted from the experience. End the gathering in prayer, asking God to bless in a special way each person who received a poinsettia during the Christmas season.

Give the Gift That Keeps on Giving. Are you tired of trying to come up with a new and unique gift for that person who has everything imaginable? If you have one of these people on your gift list, consider giving a goat, cow, or chicken to a family in need somewhere around the world in their honor. Through a ministry like Heifer International your family can provide an animal for a needy family to supply them with milk or food. When you purchase an animal from Heifer International, you are giving a struggling family a chance to become self-sufficient, which in turn can give the children of that family an education. These are only a few of the benefits when someone who has the means to do so offers someone in need the opportunity to take care of themselves and their family. Your family's gift will give a family a chance at a new future filled with hope. To get started, check out www.heifer.org for additional information about the organization and how it operates. Browse through the *Most Important Gift Catalog in the World* to determine how you, your family, or your entire church can purchase an animal. A gift can purchase a flock of geese! Partner with Heifer International to tackle the problem of hunger one family at a time by giving a renewable resource.

Teach Children the True Meaning of Giving. Are you worried that your children may not understand the true meaning of Christmas? If your children constantly talk about what they are going to get for Christmas, you may want to consider talking with them about the importance of giving. Begin your conversation by asking your children if they know what the words *charity* or *philanthropy* mean. Talk with them about how it feels to be compassionate and generous toward others. Ask them to think of a time when someone was generous to them. Have them explain how it felt when they were generous to someone else. Discuss with your children the charities in your area that are important to you. Explain what each charity does and how they help people. If possible, plan a time to take your children to different charities to look around and help out! Determine how much money you would like to donate to a charity during the Christmas season. Write a check for the amount, but leave the portion of the check where you write who the check is to blank. Ask your children to brainstorm ideas about to whom the money should be given. Once you have a list of possibilities, ask your child to choose the charity that will receive the money. Have your child fill in the check. Take your entire family to deliver the check along with a basket of fruit or a poinsettia.

Write Christmas Cards for the Elderly. For many senior adults it is a chore to write Christmas cards to their loved ones. Whether their handwriting is poor or they can't see well enough to write on a card, the task becomes a monumental one. Consider taking your older children and teenagers to a nursing home to write and address Christmas cards for the patients. Purchase Christmas cards from a discount store or ask church members to donate Christmas cards for the missions project. If you decide to go to a nursing home for the project, be sure to get permission from the director before going. If you plan to go to people's homes, call ahead to shut-ins or senior adults in your community to let them know you are coming to help them with their Christmas cards. Be sure your family has cards, writing utensils, and stamps before they get started. Encourage family members to spend time talking with the senior adult before they get started transcribing. Your family's servant heart will bring a smile to many who need a steady hand to show their love during the season.

Thank you!

Your purchase of this book and other WMU products supports the mission and ministries of WMU. To find more great resources, visit our online store at www.wmustore.com or talk with one of our friendly customer service representatives at 1-800-968-7301.

WMU®
Discover the Joy of Missions^{SM}
www.wmu.com